GW00707379

Getting Along

A comedy

Charles Mander

Samuel French—London
New York-Toronto-Hollywood

ISBN 0 573 12128 1

Please see page iv for further copyright information

CHARACTERS

Henry, ageing
Helen, middle-aged
John, middle-aged
Marcia, ageing
Norman, elderly

The action of the play passes in what is assumed to be
a gite somewhere in the South of France

Other titles by Charles Mander
published by Samuel French Ltd

Cup Final
The Deterrent
Monmouth
The River
Shop For Charity
Sparrows

GETTING ALONG

The living-room in a dilapidated gite in the Midi

The room is sparsely furnished in the French farmhouse style. There is a scrubbed wooden table, a wild collection of hard-backed chairs, a plain wooden bench, an ornate Gothic cupboard, and little else. There is a single electric bulb without a shade

The front door, positioned at an angle UR, opens directly into the room and is flanked on one side by a small shuttered window and on the other by an ornate hat and coat hanger. An open passage left of the door, also at an angle, leads to the rest of the accommodation

When the CURTAIN rises, the room is in semi-darkness, lit only by fading daylight seeping through the shutters

The closed front door is being furiously assaulted from the outside. The rattling continues for some time. The door judders and bulges as the assault becomes increasingly frenzied

Henry (*off; raging*) I can't open the bloody thing.
Helen (*off*) Are you sure it's the right place?
Henry (*off*) Of course it's the right place. Bloody thing!

The door trembles under a maddened assault

Helen (*off; anxiously*) I don't think you ought to do that. Henry, you'll damage the fittings.

Henry (*off*) You try then. Go on, you try.

Helen (*off*) I think it's a double lock. Probably has to be turned one way, then the other.

The door resists her attempts as well

Henry (*off*) Well?

Helen (*off*) If you ask me, it's not the right place. This looks more like a cowshed.

Henry (*off*) They all look like cowsheds, because they generally are cowsheds.

Helen (*off*) It didn't look like a cowshed in the brochure.

Henry (*off*) Of course not. Oh, do stop fiddling about. Give it here.

Helen (*off*) Are you sure you understood Madame's instructions, at the château? I mean your French isn't exactly…

Henry (*off*) My French is perfectly adequate, thank you.

Helen (*off*) I suppose we'll just have to go back and start again.

Norman enters from the passage, shuffling. He is a small elderly man, nattily, if somewhat eccentrically, dressed in blue slacks, a Breton shirt, and a Tyrolean hat with a large feather

Henry (*off*) I'm damned if I'll go back.

The door rattles and bangs and bulges alarmingly

Helen (*off*) Oh, do be careful, Henry.

Norman Are you trying to get in?

Henry (*off*) What?

Norman Hang on. (*He goes to the door and wrestles with the bolts*)

Henry (*off*) Who are you?
Norman What?
Henry (*off*) Now look here. We've booked this. I don't know
what you're doing in there, but this is our gite——
Helen (*off*) I think it's Norman.
Henry (*off*) Norman?
Helen (*off*) Is that you, Norman?
Norman It's me—Norman. I'm trying to unlock the door.
Henry (*off*) How the hell did you get in there?
Norman What?
Henry (*off*) Oh God. He hasn't got his hearing aid in. I said… Oh.

*Norman opens the door. We see Henry, a tall ageing man with
spindly legs, dressed in shorts and a coloured sports shirt, and
topped with a white cricketing hat*

*Helen stands beside him. She is a small, energetic woman, a few
years younger than Henry. She is dressed in a summer frock, with
a blue sun hat*

Henry and Helen enter

Norman I've been exploring.
Henry How the hell did you get in?
Norman What?

Henry grimaces

Just a moment. (*He fiddles with his hearing aid*) I think the
battery's going. Ah, that's better.
Henry (*bellowing*) I said "How did you get in?"
Norman (*clutching his ear*) Steady on! The door was open.
Henry What door?

Norman The back door.

Henry Typical. Let's get some light and air in. Place stinks of rotting cabbage. (*He makes for the window*)

Helen Let me do it. You'll probably tear out the hinges. (*She opens the shutters*)

Light floods in

Henry (*looking about himself in horror*) My God!

Norman Very—er—French.

Henry Yes, very French. (*He grimaces*)

Helen Are you sure this is the right place?

Henry Typical, typical. I could have told you.

Helen It doesn't live up to the brochure. Are you sure it's——

Henry Oh, do stop bleating, Helen. I know what I'm doing. I'm not a moron.

Norman I think there's an outside loo.

Henry That figures. (*To Helen*) What the hell made you book this place?

Helen I didn't——

Henry What?

Helen I didn't book this place… This isn't the place I booked. The place I booked was the one in the brochure. The one you fancied. Vineyards and things, handy for cheap wine, you said.

Henry Rubbish! Has anybody been upstairs?

Norman I don't think there is an upstairs.

John enters. He is a vague, balding man, a few years younger than Henry

John Hallo. I wonder if somebody could help me with Marcia. Oh… Is this the place?

Henry Yes!

John Ah.

Helen I think Henry's made a mistake.

Henry I have not made a mistake. Is there anywhere else? Did you see anywhere else on the way down?

John Er, no... Except the big building.

Henry That's the château. That's where I got the key. God, what a mess. I'm not going to live here for seven days.

John Don't you like it?

Henry Of course I don't like it.

John You didn't like the hotel either...

Helen He doesn't like anything much.

Henry I like a modicum of comfort, that's what I like, and it was seriously lacking in that hell hole we stayed in last night. I had to sit on the loo with the door open because it appeared to be constructed for midgets! I thought, at least, there'd be a little comfort here. But it seems Helen's booked a rabbit hutch. (*He glares at Helen*)

Norman moves to the door

John (*changing the subject*) Could somebody help with Marcia?

Henry What's happened to her now?

John She can't get out of the car.

Henry Stupid woman.

Helen Oh, for goodness sake, Henry.

Norman I think there's a storm brewing.

John The seat belt's jammed.

Henry That woman is a walking catastrophe. She left her bag behind in the picnic place, and we had to go back and quarter the whole area, only to find that she was sitting on the damned thing—and now she's stuck in the car. I mean you wouldn't believe... I mean...

Helen I'll go and see what I can do.

Henry Take my advice: leave her. She's better off where she is; at least she's out of the way.

Helen Sometimes you're such a bore, Henry.

Helen exits

Norman (*eagerly*) I'll go and help her.

Henry I wish you would control yourself.

Norman Pardon?

Henry You've been messing about with that woman all the way down. You're like a superannuated Lothario, and she's no better. Shrieking and giggling and putting off the drivers.

Norman Is that why you went through those lights at Rennes, and nearly knocked down that nun?

Henry (*ignoring Norman; speaking to John*) My God, this is supposed to be a holiday, we're supposed to be enjoying ourselves. What's got into Helen?

John Don't ask me. You're the husband.

John exits

Norman There's rain in the air.

Henry You haven't noticed anything funny, have you?

Norman Funny?

Henry No, you wouldn't. Too busy playing footsie with Marcia. Helen's been behaving very oddly. Snapping at me for no apparent reason.

Norman Oh—pardon?

Henry Never mind.

Norman What?

Henry You really ought to do something about that hearing aid. It's like trying to communicate with a brick wall.

Norman There's a storm brewing.

Henry (*grimacing*) Oh, God!

Henry exits through the passage

Norman gets his pipe out and stands by the door peering out

The sound of doors banging in the passage off stage

Henry enters

Henry (*returning*) Christ! There's all bunks in there. Bunks, bloody rooms stuffed with bunks.

Norman There's a storm brewing.

Henry Just wait till I see this patron or whatever he calls himself. He's breaking the Trades Description Act. I'll sue him.

Norman I don't suppose they have one in France.

Henry What?

Norman Trades description thing. Shouldn't we get our bags— er—from the car, before it rains?

Henry Why do you keep chuntering on about rain? The sun's shining. We're not in England.

Norman Oh no, we're not in England—we're in France.

Henry Well, at least you've got that straight. Congratulations. (*He glares at Norman's pipe*) You're not going to smoke that thing in here?

Norman I was going to go for a walk, but I don't like the look of the weather.

Henry Oh, for God's sake!

The sound of a distant rumble of thunder, followed by a distant shriek off stage

Norman That's thunder.

Henry Nonsense. (*He goes to the door and peers out*) There's not a cloud in the sky.

Another rumble of thunder, and another distant shriek

Ah...

Norman (*joining Henry*) You see—I was right. There's a storm brewing.

Henry What on earth is Marcia doing? You know, I sometimes think that woman is demented. She's got a rug over her head.

Norman She doesn't like thunderstorms...

Henry (*moving back from the door*) Quite honestly, I think we're all demented.

Norman Pardon?

Henry Well, we must be. There's five of us crammed into that car, in the first place. We drive miles and miles and miles through hideous tundra in acute discomfort in order to spend seven days in a clapped out gite in the middle of nowhere. We keep on doing these idiotic things, year after year, and it's always the same story. One hellish catastrophe after another. We're none of us in the first flush of youth, and some of us— (*glaring at Norman*) are in our dotage. For God's sake, we'd be better off with Saga.

Norman I was with Saga in Bulgaria——

Henry Yes, yes, I know. I know. We all know.

Norman We had to catch the coach at eight o'clock every morning—every morning. We were touring, you see. I remember, we went up to the mountains, and——

Henry Yes, I know. I'm sorry I mentioned Saga.

Norman And there was this couple from Bognor. He was—now let me think—he had been in—the wholesale food business, I think. Up in Dudley. That's in Yorkshire, you know...

Henry Shouldn't you get your bags out of the car, before it rains?

Norman No, not Staines. That was old Bill and Eileen—they came from Staines. They got lost in the monastery——
Henry I wish you'd get that damned ear-piece sorted out.

John enters, carrying a golfing brolly

John Well, we managed to disentangle Marcia.
Norman I think I'll get my bags out of the car before it rains. (*He moves towards the door; to John*) We've been talking about Bulgaria. Henry thinks we should be with Saga, and I have been telling him——
John Oh, yes, how interesting. Bulgaria...
Norman Well, I'm off to get my bags out of the car. Before it rains.

Norman exits

Henry Talking to Norman is like talking to an answerphone.
John Yes—I see what you mean. Bit of a one-way system.
Henry I was trying to tell him that in my opinion we are all demented.
John Demented?
Henry Yes. These idiotic holidays. That catastrophic boating in the Carmargue last year.
John I found it stimulating.
Henry Well, you didn't have to do anything, did you?
John I navigated, old boy.
Henry I mean physically. You didn't have to risk life and limb leaping about and hauling on ropes.
John Oh, that.
Henry I know, I know. You've got two hernias and a heart condition. Norman's stone deaf, and Marcia is about as much use as the walking dead. Which left Helen and me to do all the pushing and shoving, and we're not exactly youthful. It took

me three months to recover last year. Three months! It's
madness. We ought to be relaxing in a comfortable hotel, and
strolling about in straw hats and linen jackets. We're too old for
this sort of malarkey.

John Think young. Think young, Henry. If you don't speculate,
you won't accumulate.

Henry What the hell has that got to do with it?

John Life's a challenge.

Henry Do you always express yourself in clichés?

John It just sprang to mind, that's all. Besides, I thought we
managed the boat pretty well, all things considered.

Henry It was a disaster. And this is a disaster as well. All our
holidays are disasters.

John Oh, I think they're terrific fun.

Henry I don't call it terrific fun, cramped five in a car with
Norman and Marcia groping each other. I call it torture.

John He is a bit persistent.

Henry Persistent? He's rabid.

John I suppose it's because he lives alone.

Henry Well, you live alone, and I don't see you... Which
reminds me. Helen's getting peculiar.

John How do you mean?

Henry She called me a bore just now.

John Oh, did she?

Henry Yes.

John Ah.

Henry These damned holidays. She becomes very neurotic.

John Really?

Henry Yes. Haven't you noticed?

John No.

Henry (*significantly*) No, you wouldn't...

John Well, we can all relax, now we're here.

The sound of distant gunshots off stage

Henry Relax? Look at this place. Look at it! It's about as relaxing as a station waiting room. And there's bunks in the bedroom. Bunks.

Helen and Marcia enter. Marcia is a round, excitable woman. She has a rug over her head

Helen We made it. Did you hear the gun shots?

Henry They shoot everything in this country—everything. There's not a damned thing they don't shoot, except magpies.

Helen It's going to rain.

Henry They shoot tourists as well, when they're not hammering them over the head with meat cleavers. Does she have to go about with a rug over her head?

Marcia (*in a trembling and muffled voice*) I do hope this isn't going to develop. If it gets bad, I may have to go into a cupboard.

Henry A cupboard? What on earth for?

Helen She doesn't like thunderstorms, lots of people don't.

A distant rumble off stage. Marcia shrieks

It's all right, Marcia. That was miles away.

Marcia It's so savage, so primeval. I can't stand loud noises. I'm highly strung.

Helen If we close the shutters you won't see the lightning. (*She goes to the window*)

Henry Oh, God. I suppose we'll have to crouch about in the dark.

Helen You can turn the light on.

Marcia I'd feel safer in a cupboard.

Helen (*pulling at the shutters*) Wouldn't that be uncomfortable?

Marcia No, I'd be happier in a cupboard.

Henry Oh, put her in a cupboard, if that's what she wants.

Helen (*sharply*) That's enough, Henry.

Henry Well, it's what she wants, isn't it? It's what she wants. Put her in there! (*He marches to the cupboard and sweeps open a door*)

Crockery tumbles out of the cupboard in an avalanche. Marcia jumps and shrieks. She crumples to the floor and sits there

Helen Now look what you've done. (*To Marcia; soothingly*) It's all right, Marcia. Henry's just smashed a dinner service, that's all.

Henry begins to fling plates back into the cupboard

John Here, let me help. (*He joins Henry*)
Henry Bloody things!
Helen Well, it's your own fault. Stupid thing to do.

A rumble of thunder off stage. Marcia shrieks

Henry Do you have to make that noise?
Marcia Yes... Yes—I'm sorry.
John (*getting up*) I'll see if there's a broom cupboard under the stairs.
Henry There aren't any stairs.
John Well, I'll look anyway. (*He moves towards the passage*)
Helen That's very thoughtful of you, John. I wish my husband would be half as thoughtful as you. You are a gentleman.
John (*embarrassed*) Thank you. Er, thank you.

John exits

Henry (*bristling*) Just what exactly do you mean by that?
Helen I would have thought the meaning was obvious. Even to you.

Henry No, it is not!

Helen You're becoming a bore, Henry. You do nothing but moan. We're sick of it. We're all sick of it.

A rumble of thunder off stage. Marcia shrieks

Henry Why does she have to do that?

Helen Because she's frightened of thunder, that's why. Lots of people are frightened of thunder. Stop going on about it.

Two shots off stage, louder and closer than before. Marcia shrieks

Henry This is hell! I'm going to lie down. (*He stalks towards the passage*)

Helen What about the bags?

Henry They can stay where they are. As soon as this storm has passed, I intend to go in search of a decent hotel, if such a thing exists in this God-forsaken place.

John enters

Henry knocks into him, as he hurries to the door and exits

John Oh, so sorry, er...

Helen It's he that should apologize. He needs bonking on the head! If he hates it so much, why doesn't he stay at home? I could stock up the freezer.

Another rumble of thunder, and another shriek from Marcia

Helen Oh, do shut up, Marcia. It's miles away.

John There is a sort of cupboard, in the passage.

Marcia (*emotionally*) Thank God! Will you take me there? (*She struggles to her feet and blunders about blindly*)

John (*leading her*) I'm afraid you'll find it a bit stuffy.

Marcia I don't mind. Just so long as I can't see the flashes and I can keep my ears blocked.

John and Marcia exit

Helen opens the shutters. Grey light filters in

Norman enters. He is lugging an enormous suitcase on wheels

Norman It's rumbling round the hills. There's a man out there with a gun. I took my hat off. (*He shows her his feathered hat*)

Helen Ah... Very wise.

Norman Best to be on the safe side. I think I'll assemble my Teasmade; always take it with me. Hungary, Bulgaria, Germany; always take my Teasmade. Can't stand a day without a cuppa. (*He lugs his case towards the passage*)

John enters

John I can't think she'll be very comfortable, but there it is.

Norman Romania, Turkey...

Norman exits

Helen He's becoming an awful bore.

John He does rather go on.

Helen Henry, I mean.

John Oh.

Helen He really has become a bore. (*She starts to weep*)

John Well, er, she won't be able to get out. When the time comes. Cupboard only opens from the outside. Oh, I say...

Helen collapses into a chair

Helen (*weeping*) Never wants to go out these days. Rude to all my friends. Never stops complaining, and now he's lying down.

John I expect he's tired, you know. Not much sleep, in the hotel... Er...

Helen Rubbish! He slept like a log, he always does.

John Ah...

Helen He doesn't even read.

John (*embarrassed*) Really?

Helen Goes out like a light. I might as well not be there. It's like being married to a railway sleeper. How I've put up with it for thirty-five years I don't know. I just don't know. I wish I'd married you.

John Pardon?

Helen You were his best man.

John Yes, but...

Helen (*jumping up*) Oh, forget it! Is that man still shooting?

John I expect so.

Helen Norman took his hat off. I think he thought he might be mistaken for a pheasant or something.

John Pheasant?

Helen All those feathers. (*She turns to him*) Better not tell anybody—what I said just now.

John I wouldn't dream of it.

Helen No, I'm sure you wouldn't.

John Of course not.

Henry You see, it's just that I so look forward to these holidays, and he has to ruin them. I think about them for months; it's the only thing that keeps me going. Life is so... So hum-drum, now the children have grown up. I sometimes wonder if it has any purpose at all.

John One soldiers on...

Helen I mean, I don't honestly think Henry would notice if I left
  him. He'd wonder why the food wasn't coming, but I don't
  think he'd miss me.

John He would, you know.

Helen Do you really think so?

John Oh yes... (*Sadly*) Oh yes.

Helen Oh, Lord. I've brought it all back, haven't I?

John It never went.

Helen God, it's so unfair.

John Yes, on the face of it, yes. She didn't suffer much pain, it
  was quick and that's a blessing.

Helen You miss her very much. Don't you?

John Of course—lost without her. It's the same with the others.
  Not Henry, because he has you. But the others...

Helen I know.

John I mean, putting love on one side. There's the companionship, the dependency. When that's gone...

Henry I suppose that's why Norman is always going off with
  Saga.

John Yes. Bulgaria, Romania...

Helen (*laughing*) Hungary, Turkey. And Marcia?

John Utterly lost. We're all three of us cripples in different ways.
  Going into old age is not always a happy experience. Going
  there alone can be a bloody awful experience. That's why these
  holidays are so important. Companionship, you see.

Helen Yes. Companionship...

John Mind you, we're very lucky. We're very lucky to have the
  money to do this. So many don't, so many live on in poverty,
  die in poverty, unmourned, unnoticed, forgotten. We're very
  lucky. (*He brightens up*) And above all, we're very lucky to
  have you, Helen.

Helen Oh, nonsense.

John We depend on you. We all depend on you.

Helen Because I speak French?

John Yes, but more than that. You have a sort of practical compassion, very rare in this day and age.

Helen Oh... Well, I'm afraid I don't feel very compassionate at the moment. (*She smiles*) Present company excepted, of course. In fact, I feel quite the opposite. I feel exceedingly put upon and I'm surprised you don't feel that as well.

John Henry?

Helen Oh yes, Henry—and the others. I mean, he goes to bed. The moment we arrive, Henry goes to bed.

John Perhaps we should get the supplies in.

Helen No. Will you run me up to the château?

John Now?

Helen Yes. I'm sure this isn't our gite.

John Well, I wondered that, but Henry seemed so certain.

Helen Henry needs treatment. He needs shaking out of his damnable self-complacency. He has a sort of Lord-God-Almighty complex. I'm fed up with it. Come on.

John What about the others?

Helen What about them?

John Shouldn't we tell them?

Helen No. They'll only want to come. I'm a bit sick of them all at the moment. Let's sneak off quietly.

John That's a bit naughty.

Helen I feel naughty.

John If Henry finds us gone, he'll jump to all sorts of conclusions.

Helen Such as?

John Well, er, you know. I mean...

Helen Us? (*She laughs*) Good heavens.

John I think he's a bit suspicious.

Helen Nonsense. I'm merely an appendage to Henry. He's much too self-centred to have those sort of suspicions.

John They're expecting us to get them a meal, Helen.

Helen Exactly. They expect us to do everything.

John What about the supplies, shouldn't we bring them in?

Helen No. We must go now while we have the chance. They can feast on Norman's Frosties if they get hungry, and we won't be long. (*She goes to the door*) Come on.

John I still think he might jump to conclusions.

Helen Splendid. I hope he does.

John (*picking up his brolly*) I see what you mean about not feeling compassionate.

Helen I just want to get away from Henry's self-centred moaning, Marcia's shrieking and dithering, and Norman's Saga experiences for a little while. Come on.

Helen and John exit furtively

Norman enters with his Teasmade

Norman Well, here we are, all we need is a suitable electric plug. It fitted the plugs in Bulgaria and Romania, so I daresay… (*He looks around; puzzled*) Oh, vanished. (*He goes to the window and peers out*)

Henry enters, storming

Henry My God, those bunks! I'd be better off on a gridiron. I'm going to look for a hotel.

Norman Pardon?

Henry Oh, never mind.

Henry stalks to the door

The sound of a car driving away off stage

(*Bellowing off*) Hoy! (*He turns back inside*) Some bastard's making off with our car!

Norman Just a moment. (*He fiddles with his hearing aid*)
Henry Where are the others?
Norman Pardon?
Henry I said "Where are the others?" (*He shouts*) Helen? Helen?
Marcia (*off; in a muffled voice*) Is it over?
Norman What?

Henry rushes to the door to peer out

Henry Good God! (*He turns around*) Where the hell is Helen?
  She must call the police.
Norman (*still fiddling with his hearing aid*) Helen?
Henry Yes... (*Into Norman's ear-piece*) Hallo! Testing. Mary
  had a little lamb——
Norman (*clutching his ear*) Steady on. You'll break it. Helen
  isn't here.
Henry Yes, I know that. I know that.
Norman She went off in the car.
Henry What?
Norman What?
Marcia (*off*) Hallo. Can I come out, please?

The sound of knocks and thumps off stage

Norman (*regaining contact*) What's that?
Henry Never mind. Helen went off in the car. Is that what you're
  saying?
Norman Er, yes.
Henry On her own?
Norman It was all so quick, and sort of furtive.
Henry Furtive?

The sound of banging and thumping off stage

Marcia (*off*) Help!

Henry How do you mean, furtive?

Norman They went off furtively.

Henry They?

Norman (*vaguely*) There was a man... I think. I only caught a glimpse, you see. I was looking for a connection for this. (*He holds up the Teasmade*) I always carry it with me. Been to Bulgaria, Hungary, Germany——

Henry Yes, yes, yes, along with your breakfast Frosties and Cup-a-Soup. I know all about it, I've heard it a hundred times! What man?

Norman Pardon?

Henry (*bellowing*) What man? Was it John?

Norman Well, it might have been. On the other hand...

Henry What?

Norman It might have been the gunman.

Henry Gunman?

Marcia (*off*) Help! *Help!*

Norman Is that somebody in distress?

Henry What do you mean—gunman?

Norman Well, he was carrying a gun, or it might have been an umbrella, but it could have been a gun. So it could have been the gunman... Out there, shooting things. Bang—bang! I took my hat off.

Henry You're talking gibberish.

Norman Pardon?

Henry (*shouting*) Are you trying to tell me that my wife has been abducted by a French gunman—in our car?

Norman I shouldn't think so.

Henry Then what are you trying to tell me?

Norman Perhaps they've gone shopping.

Henry Helen and the French gunman?

Norman Well, yes... But very furtively.

Henry (*grimacing*) Gordon Bennett!

Marcia (*off*) Please let me out. It's very hot in here. I am not well!

Henry Oh, for God's sake, let her out!

Norman Who?

Henry Marcia, of course. She's in a cupboard.

Norman A what?

Henry Are you trying to cover up?

Norman Did you say that Marcia was in a cupboard?

Henry She's gone off with John. Bloody well jaunted off—that's what's happened. Just gone off. Left me here with two geriatric lunatics and no food. (*He stalks up and down*) Oh, thank you! Thank you very much!

A crash of splintering wood, followed by shrieks from Marcia, off stage

Norman Er, I think——

Henry Oh, yes, I can see it now. I can see it all now. Crystal clear! They've been plotting this for months. I never did trust that damned Lothario. Loafing about on that bloody boat last year and rutting after Helen. Now he's abducted her. The swine! The fornicating swine! Jaunting off with my wife and the luggage. I suppose we won't get any lunch!

Marcia enters, staggering. She is adorned with bits of wood and dust

What the hell are you doing?

Marcia (*tearfully*) I'm... I'm not very well.

Norman Oh, my word. Here, sit down.

Marcia (*weeping*) Oh, dear. I thought I would die. So hot, so... Has the thunder gone?

Norman If I can find a connection, I could make a cup of tea.

Marcia I burst out. I simply burst out. I thought I would die. Has the storm passed?

Henry Yes, yes.

Marcia (*looking around*) Where's Helen?

Henry She's gone.

Marcia (*alarmed*) Helen gone? Gone where?

Henry Well, I don't know. How should I know? I'm the last person to know. I'm just an inconvenience.

Norman (*searching about for a plug*) A plug, a plug, my kingdom for a plug.

Henry They've gone off in the car with a gunman, according to Norman, but you can't depend on what he says because he's totally deaf and lives in Bulgaria.

Norman Bulgaria? Do you know I went there last year, with Saga——

Henry Shut up! They've gone off with all the food and the bags, and they probably won't be coming back.

Marcia I expect they've gone shopping.

Henry We went shopping this morning. We spent hours and hours shopping, there was enough food in that car to feed an army. So why should they want to go shopping again?

Norman (*spotting a plug*) Hey-ho! Eureka!

Marcia Perhaps they've gone swimming.

Henry Don't be ridiculous.

Marcia I hope they won't be away for long. I don't feel very secure without Helen. She's... She's so positive and *simpatico*, such a prop in an uncertain world. Are we going to have lunch?

Henry No, we are not going to have lunch. There's nothing to have lunch with.

Norman I've got a packet of soup.

Henry No, thank you!

Norman I found it a life saver in Bulgaria, you know. Did I ever tell you——

Henry Oh, for God's sake, shut up about Bulgaria! (*He puts his hand to his throat*) I've had it up to here with Bulgaria.

Norman (*adjusting his hearing aid*) What?

Henry And throw that bloody thing away. You don't need it.

Norman Pardon?

Henry (*shouting*) I said "You don't need a hearing aid." You don't need ears. You never listen to anything but your own voice. You're simplex, you only work in the transmitting position.

Marcia Perhaps they've gone to get a postcard.

Henry Oh God!

Henry exits in a fury

Marcia (*to Norman*) You don't really think they've been taken hostage, do you?

Norman (*grinning*) No. I only said it to wind him up. Give him something to moan about. I mean, really moan about. Although it could have been the gunman—if it wasn't an umbrella. Would you like a cup of tea when it comes up?

Marcia If there's one going. But you must be a good boy. (*She giggles coquettishly*)

Norman (*advancing on her*) Go on, you love it.

Marcia No, Norman. No! Now stop it. Be serious.

Norman tickles her

Ahh! Stop it!

She smacks his hand away

Go and make the tea.

Norman (*desisting and moving to the Teasmade*) It makes itself, that's the glory of it. Gives you time for other things.

Norman advances on Marcia again

Marcia Stop it! You're a pestiferous old goat.

She beats him away

   He really seems put out.
Norman Who?
Marcia Henry.
Norman He shouts so much, I can hardly hear what he says. It
   jams my hearing aid. I think he thinks that Helen and John have
   done a runner.
Marcia They wouldn't. I mean, surely, they wouldn't.
Norman Well, you never know. It's a funny old world. (*He
   advances upon her again*)
Marcia Get away! Get away! Why do you keep assaulting me?
Norman Because you like it.
Marcia No, I don't. That Teasmade isn't working.
Norman Yes, it is.
Marcia No, it isn't. You feel it. I bet it's cold.

Norman goes over and bends down to feel the Teasmade

Norman Blimey, it is cold. Blimey—Ha!

Marcia hops to him and pinches his bottom

Norman (*yelping and kicking over the Teasmade*) Gerroff!
Marcia Got you! (*She giggles hugely and moves away from him*)
Norman Look what you've made me do. Right—you've asked
   for it. (*He trots after her*)
Marcia (*shrieking hugely*) No! *No!*

*She lets him catch her and he tickles her, making her shriek and
giggle*

Henry enters

Henry What the hell are you playing at?

Marcia Nothing.

Henry You were groping about. You're always fingering that woman. It's disgusting.

Norman (*adjusting his hearing aid*) What?

Henry I said "It's disgusting." Especially in the circumstances.

Norman What circumstances?

Henry You can't keep your hands to yourself, can you? God help all those women in Saga.

Marcia We were filling in the time.

Norman Enjoying ourselves. That's what we are here for, to enjoy ourselves.

Henry At your age? Don't be ridiculous.

Norman (*with dignity*) Age has nothing to do with it. Because we're senior citizens it doesn't mean to say that we can't let our hair down from time to time. You ought to try it.

Henry Certainly not!

Norman It might make you a little less dismal.

Henry I am not dismal!

Norman Oh, you are! You are! You're dismal, and that's a fact.

Henry How come you can suddenly hear every word I say now?

Norman (*adjusting his hearing aid*) What?

Marcia (*changing the subject*) Did you find Helen?

Henry Does it look like it?

Marcia Er, no.

Henry How can she do this to me? How can she do it?

Norman She may have been kidnapped. They may both have been kidnapped. It's not unknown in foreign places. Come to think of it, one of our ladies on my last Saga tour to Bulgaria— she went missing and all they said——

Henry Oh, shut up!

Norman No, they said she could have been kidnapped. But as it turned out——

Marcia (*alarmed*) What? What?

Norman She was stuck in the lift, between two floors. They had to get the courier, and the courier had to get the manager, and the manager had to call the fire brigade, but the telephones didn't work. So, er, I think she got out in the end. Yes, she got out, in the end, because she was on the coach when we went up the mountain…

Marcia Oh, my word, Norman. You do lead an exciting life. Oh, I do envy you, getting about. Seeing the world.

Henry (*beating his forehead*) Oh God!

Henry exits into the passage

Norman Have to do something, you know. Keep occupied. No good sitting at home moping. So I quest about, always on the move. I've been to Russia.

Marcia Russia? I don't think I'd like that. You must be very wealthy.

Norman Bit put away. We always wanted to see the world, Sylvia and me. Saved up for it. I saw a bit when I was in the army during the war, but she never did—and now she's dead and never will. But I go on. I go on. (*He looks desolate for a moment*)

Marcia We used to go to Italy. Every year to Italy. Same place. George spoke three languages, but we always went to Italy. It was his great love. I relied on him, depended on him. Now I depend on Helen. I wish I could be independent, like you.

Norman Henry's lucky. He may not think he is. But he is. (*To himself; quietly*) Lucky bastard.

Marcia Yes, he's lucky. Lucky to have Helen. I wish I could have her.

Norman You what?

Marcia Not like that—you are a one. You've got a funny mind, Norman. I mean... Well, I find it difficult to cope.

Norman You need a man.

Marcia This will be my last holiday. Nothing left in the kitty. I've so enjoyed them—in spite of everything.

Norman So have I. Much the best sort of holiday. Saga's all right, but... Well, it's friendship—being able to let your hair down, with friends. He thinks I'm a bore. I go on, you see, about Bulgaria, and... Well, I go on.

Marcia I don't think you're a bore.

Norman Well, you're special. They don't understand that, do they?

Marcia Who?

Norman Them. (*He nods around vaguely*) They don't understand and they don't care. I'm deaf, see. So I'm stupid; anybody who's deaf is stupid. I got this in the war. (*He taps his ear*) Bloody shell... But they don't care—water under the bridge. Nobody cares when you're old... Water under the bridge... They don't know what it was like. And they don't care.

Marcia George was in the war.

Norman Well, he's dead now, isn't he.

Marcia Yes... He's dead.

Norman So, he's all right, isn't he?

Marcia He used to shout at me a lot, but I didn't mind—you get used to it. I miss him.

Norman Yes... Can I ask you something?

Marcia Is it personal?

Norman Yes.

Marcia Oh.

Norman Have you considered matrimony?

Marcia Matrimony?

Norman Yes, matrimony—getting hitched.

Marcia Oh no, once is enough for me, quite enough, thank you.

Norman Only I thought that if you was… Well, I'm free.

Marcia You? (*She giggles nervously*) Don't be daft.

Norman Why not? I mean, we're both… Well…

Marcia Oh no. No, I couldn't manage Saga. And, well, I'm set in my ways. (*Earnestly*) You see, I'm in the Oxfam shop every Thursday.

Norman What's that got to do with getting hitched?

Marcia (*staggering up*) I think I'll go and watch for Helen.

Norman Are you turning me down?

Marcia Well, I've had a hip job… I'm set in my ways. Not very quick on my feet. (*She totters to the door*)

Norman I'll come with you.

Marcia (*helplessly*) Oh.

Henry enters, stealing in from the passage

Henry (*beckoning to Norman*) Psst!

Norman (*creaking on to one knee; half-seriously*) Will you marry me, Marcia?

Marcia Oh, oh!

Henry Pssst!

Marcia (*relieved*) Oh, hullo, Henry.

Norman Marry me, Marcia, please, while I'm in the mood.

Henry (*hoarsely*) Keep your voice down!

Norman What?

Henry grimaces

Marcia I'll go and watch out for Helen.

Marcia exits

Norman struggles off his creaking knees

Henry What on earth are you doing now?

Norman Nothing.

Henry You were proposing marriage. (*He drags Norman to his feet*) Bit old for that, aren't you?

Norman (*with dignity*) Certainly not.

Henry Keep your voice down! Down. (*He gestures with his hands*)

Norman But I've just got up. Is this a game?

Henry No. (*He looks round furtively*) There's somebody in the kitchen.

Norman (*adjusting his hearing aid*) Can you speak up a bit?

Henry (*maddened*) Hell's teeth!

Norman Teeth? (*He puts his hand to his mouth*) They're all right, I think. What's the problem?

Henry (*articulating hoarsely*) There is somebody in the kitchen.

Norman Oh. There's somebody in the kitchen. Who?

Henry I don't know. There's two of them and one of them has a gun.

Norman A gun?

Henry Yes.

Norman Oh, oh, are you sure?

Henry Of course I'm sure. I had to take avoiding action.

Norman Why?

Henry Because they looked exceedingly unwholesome. Scruffy, foreign.

Norman French?

Henry Yes, one might assume that, since we happen to be in France.

Norman Only, you said foreign...

Henry Well, natives, then. Natives.

Norman Because, you see, you can't call them foreign if they happen to be French in France. In France, we're foreign, if you see what I mean.

Henry Yes, yes, no need to labour it. Damn, where the hell is

Helen? (*He hurries to the window and peers out*) She's no
business to go off like that and leave us here—surrounded by
gunmen.

Norman Perhaps they're cleaners.

Henry Cleaners? I told you that one of them had a gun. You don't
take a gun about when you go cleaning, not even in France.
They're up to no good. Don't you read the papers?

Norman What papers?

Henry The papers! Bloody gunmen, murdering tourists. French
farmers mutilating sheep.

Norman (*enjoying himself*) Oh, French farmers. Well, they could
very well be French farmers or bandits. It couldn't be the other
gunman because he went off in the car with Helen and John.

Henry (*highly agitated*) Bloody place! Why did she have to
choose this bloody bandit-infested place in the middle of
nowhere, and then jaunt off and leave us defenceless. They'll
murder us for our belongings. They're always doing that in
France.

Norman When I was in Russia with Saga, we went on the Trans-
Siberian railway, you now. In each carriage there was a big
woman, a babushka. Fearsome——

Henry Look, I don't think you quite understand——

Norman That's what we need now. A big fearsome woman, a
babushka.

Henry We haven't got a big fearsome woman, have we?

Norman (*tentatively*) Marcia.

Henry Look, this isn't funny. It isn't funny.

Norman The bandits kept well away from the babushkas, I can
tell you that.

Henry (*tiptoeing over and listening in the passage*) Listen! Do
you hear anything?

Norman (*adjusting his hearing aid*) What?

Henry Oh, forget it. We must call the police. Is there a telephone?

Norman Er, there might be one in the kitchen.

Henry Well, that's very useful. Very useful indeed.

Norman Of course, if we were with Saga, we could call the courier.

Henry We're not with Saga. We're not with Saga. Can't you get it into your thick head? We are not with Saga!

Norman I thought you said to keep our voices down.

Henry (*whispering*) I did. I did!

Norman What?

Henry (*going to pieces*) Oh, Christ in heaven! Why isn't Helen here? I don't know what to do. I don't know what to do.

Norman Tell you what. I'll sort them out. I still have my unarmed combat. (*He moves purposefully towards the passage*)

Henry No!

Norman Why not?

Henry Because they'd have you for breakfast, and me too. We don't want to call attention to ourselves. They might not know we're here.

Norman I wouldn't have thought that was likely. You've been making enough noise to wake the dead.

Henry Listen!

Norman What?

Henry I said, "Listen!"

The sound of shuffling footsteps in the passage off stage

They're coming.

Norman Pardon?

Henry I'm getting out of here. (*He rushes to the door*)

A car is heard approaching off stage. Henry hurtles back

My God! The bastards, they've got us surrounded. (*He tries to get into the crockery cupboard. The china flies out with a crash*)

Marcia enters. She is holding a glass of wine in her hand

Marcia (*to Henry*) Oh, dear. Has the thunder come back?

Henry How the hell did you…? Where have you been?

Marcia I walked round and came in through the kitchen.

Henry Kitchen?

Marcia Were you getting into the cupboard?

Henry Er, no.

Marcia Well, that's a relief. Thought it was the thunder. I've got a glass of wine. Two nice young people—French, but they could speak English—offered me a glass of wine. Cheers.

Henry You fool!

Marcia I beg your pardon?

Henry They're up to no good. Didn't you realize that? Didn't you see the gun?

Marcia Oh yes. He was cleaning it. He'd got three starlings and a sparrow, I think. I averted my eyes. They were quite surprised when I walked in.

Norman Henry thinks they're bandits.

Marcia Oh, dear me. (*She giggles*) Bandits? Oh, dear me.

Henry (*furiously*) I didn't say they were bandits. (*To Norman*) You said they were bandits. I said they were up to no good. Who are they? Did you ask?

Marcia Er, no.

Henry You just blundered in, accepted a glass of wine, and didn't ask them what the hell they thought they were doing in our gite?

Marcia I don't think it is our gite.

Henry What do you mean? It's our gite, we booked it, for God's sake. What do you mean?

Marcia I wish Helen was here. I don't like it when you shout at me like that, it reminds me of my late husband.

Henry Well, I'm sorry, but you none of you realize the trauma that I've been through. You could have walked into a nest of gunmen.

Marcia What?

Henry You heard what I said. You heard what I said. Are you completely demented?

Norman Now look here.

Henry Don't you threaten me! What are they up to? That's what I'd like to know. What the hell are they up to? (*To Marcia*) Well, go on, what were they up to? Didn't you engage them in conversation? Demand an explanation?

Marcia Yes... No. They were concerned. Said they thought I might find it a bit rough here, that I was a bit old for the grapes. So there's no need to shout. But I don't think this is our gite. I wish Helen was here. (*She weeps*)

Norman There, there. Weepy, weepy.

He hugs her

Marcia (*petulantly*) Oh, go away!

She beats him off

Henry They've no business to be cleaning their guns and doling out wine in our gite.

Helen and John enter

Helen It's not our gite.

Henry Who said that?

Helen It's not our gite, Henry. We stopped off at the château.

Henry You're back. Well, that's something. You've no idea what's been happening. It's been hell! Why didn't you tell me you were jaunting off?

Helen We didn't think you'd notice.

Henry Of course I noticed!

Helen You were asleep, so John and I thought we'd slip off.

Henry Jaunt off. Jaunt off and leave me alone with these two. I think that's despicable. (*To John*) I know what your game is, and I don't like it.

Helen Don't tell me you're jealous, Henry.

Marcia So glad you're back, Helen, so glad. I had to break out of that cupboard, and Henry's been shouting at me, and Norman keeps proposing. (*She weeps*) It's been terrible, terrible.

Henry (*to John; ferociously*) If you were twenty years younger, I'd lay you out!

Norman (*leaping after Marcia*) Marry me, petal, and we'll quest the world together.

Marcia (*hysterically*) You see! You see!

Henry You leave my wife alone! Leave her alone!

John Yes, all right, all right.

Helen That's enough, Henry. That's quite enough!

Henry No, it isn't. You realize that there are two bloody Frenchmen in our kitchen and one of them has a gun. Christ, we could have been murdered for all you cared!

Helen We're in France, for goodness sake, not outer Mongolia.

Norman Outer Mongolia? I'm thinking of going there next summer. I think Saga run——

Helen Yes, I think it would be a good idea if you transferred your suitcase to the car, Norman. Perhaps John could give you a hand.

Henry Now what the hell are you up to?

Helen If you'd like to go with them, Marcia…

Marcia Oh, all right, but I don't want him to keep proposing, it's worse than tickling.

Norman Go on, you love it! (*He advances on her*)

Helen Don't forget your Teasmade.

Norman Oh, Teasmade. Yes, can't do without that. Goes everywhere with me: Romania, Hungary, Russia, Bulgaria. (*To Marcia*) We'll take this on our honeymoon.

Marcia Ugh!

Marcia and John exit through the door

Norman exits through the passage with his Teasmade

Helen You see, this isn't our gite. It isn't a gite at all. It's a bunkhouse for grape pickers.

Henry What do you mean?

Helen I thought it was the wrong place. It bore no resemblance to the brochure.

Henry But...

Helen So we called in to the château. Apparently the owner was out—shooting, but Madame was there. She'd wondered why we had set out in the wrong direction in the first place after she had explained so carefully.

Henry But I understood, I mean... Well, why didn't you come in with me?

Helen Because I think you'd forgotten I was there.

Henry (*indignantly*) No, I hadn't.

Helen I don't think you notice me.

Henry Of course I notice you. I...

Helen Anyway, the real gite is the other side of the vineyard. John and I had a look and it's very nice indeed. So I suggest we get over there. Right? (*She moves to the door*)

Henry Oh, right, er...

Helen Yes?

Norman enters, dragging his case behind him

Norman We could do with a courier or a babushka or both. (*He moves to the door*)

Helen opens the door for him

Ta. (*Turning in the doorway*) Give me this any day to Saga. It's the companionship, you see, adventure. Jolly friends all together. Here I come, Marcia. You know you love it.

Norman exits

A distant shriek from Marcia off stage

Henry Jolly friends, eh? I could think of other words for it.

Helen They're lonely people. Come to think of it, we're all lonely people, though I can't speak for you.

Henry We're not lonely. We have each other.

Helen Do we, Henry? Do we?

Henry Well, yes. Oh, hell... John.

Helen It passed my mind, Henry. So, a little bit of advice: don't take anyone for granted, not even your wife.

Henry I don't take you for granted. What makes you think that?

Helen Because, when you're not moaning at me, you ignore me. When was the last time you took me out to dinner?

Henry (*indignantly*) How can I take you out to dinner when you're always hemmed in by John and those demented geriatrics? I can never get a look in.

Helen I don't think that's the point.

Henry It is the point. Heavens above! Why can't we just go away together? Why do we always have to travel with this entourage?

Helen Because it gives them pleasure and it gives me somebody to talk to.

Henry I talk to you.

Helen You go on—that's not talking. That's moaning. I doubt whether you've actually talked to me since we were courting.

Henry What rubbish! I'm always talking to you. You're my wife. I love you, Helen.

Helen Then show it.

Henry What?
Helen Show it.
Henry Oh... Right.

He kisses her fiercely

How's that?
Helen Ah... That's more like it.
Henry (*jealously*) I bet John can't kiss like that.
Helen I wouldn't know.
Henry Is that the truth?
Helen Yes.
Henry Well, that's a relief. I thought, I really thought...
Helen He said you'd jump to conclusions, and you did. You've
been jumping to conclusions all over the place. Gunmen in the
kitchen! (*She laughs*)
Henry (*seriously*) I need you, Helen. I really do. I don't take you
for granted. I...
Helen We ought to go now. The others will be waiting.
Henry (*jealously*) The others! Oh, yes, we mustn't keep the
others waiting.
Helen No, we mustn't.
Henry Why the hell do you do it, Helen? Why?
Helen Because I want to help them, and because, maybe, one day,
one of us will be in the same position, and I would like to think
that there might be somebody around who cares. Come on.
Henry All right, all right.
Helen If only you would stop going on, Henry, and start getting
on, it would be so much easier.
Henry Getting on? Ha! I would have thought that was inevitable.
Helen In one sense, yes. But in the other sense it is fairly vital if
life is to be worth living. Why not try it?
Henry I do get on.

Helen Do you?
Henry Of course.

A car horn sounds off stage

(*Shouting irritably*) All right, we're coming! Hell's teeth! Can't you leave me alone with my wife for three minutes without hooting? Bloody entourage.
Helen See what I mean?
Henry Oh, shut up!

Helen looks at him sharply, but Henry is grinning

Helen Come on.

They exit, as——

——the CURTAIN *falls*

FURNITURE AND PROPERTY LIST

On stage: Scrubbed wooden table
Hard-backed chairs
Plain wooden bench
Ornate Gothic cupboard. *In it:* crockery
Electric bulb
Ornate hat and coat hanger
Electric socket

Off stage: Golfing umbrella (**John**)
Rug (**Marcia**)
Suitcase on wheels (**Norman**)
Teasmade (**Norman**)
Glass of wine (**Marcia**)

Personal: **Norman:** hearing aid, pipe

LIGHTING PLOT

Property fittings requred: one bare light bulb
Interior. The same throughout

To open: Fading daylight effect, seeping in through the window shutters

Cue 1   **Helen** opens the shutters   (Page 4)
         Increase the daylight effect

Cue 2   **Helen** pulls the shutters shut   (Page 11)
         Fade down the daylight effect

Cue 3   **Helen** opens the shutters   (Page 14)
         Bring up grey daylight effect

EFFECTS PLOT

Cue 1   **Norman** gets his pipe out   (Page 7)
Sound of doors banging

Cue 2   **Henry:** "Oh, for God's sake!"   (Page 7)
Distant thunder

Cue 3   **Henry:** "…not a cloud in the sky."   (Page 8)
Distant thunder

Cue 4   **John:** "…now we're here."   (Page 10)
Distant gunshots

Cue 5   **Helen:** "…lots of people don't."   (Page 11)
Distant rumble

Cue 6   **Helen:** "Stupid thing to do."   (Page 12)
Rumble of thunder

Cue 7   **Helen:** "We're all sick of it."   (Page 13)
Rumble of thunder

Cue 8   **Helen:** "Stop going on about it."   (Page 13)
Two shots, closer than before

Cue 9   **Helen:** "…stock up the freezer."   (Page 13)
Rumble of thunder

Cue 10   **Henry** stalks to the door   (Page 18)
Sound of a car driving away

Cue 11	**Marcia**: (*off*) "…Can I come out, please?"	(Page 19)
	Knocks and thumps	
Cue 12	**Henry**: "Furtive?"	(Page 19)
	Banging and thumping	
Cue 13	**Henry**: "Thank you very much!"	(Page 21)
	Crash of splintering wood	
Cue 14	**Henry**: "I said, 'Listen!'"	(Page 31)
	Shuffling footsteps	
Cue 15	**Henry**: "I'm getting out of here."	(Page 31)
	Sound of an approaching car	
Cue 16	**Henry**: "Of course."	(Page 38)
	Car horn